The Power of the
LMS 2-6-0s

Hughes/Fowler 'Crab' 2-6-0 No 42924 of Longsight shed, Manchester, pilots Patricroft 'Jubilee' No 45558 *Manitoba* out of Leeds City on a Summer Saturday relief to the regular 9.55am Newcastle–Liverpool on 20 August 1960. This locomotive would last until February 1966, by which time only around 20 examples remained in service. *Gavin Morrison*

One of 22 Ivatt '4MTs' allocated new
to New England shed, Peterborough,
No 43082 was still based there on
19 June 1954, when it was
photographed leaving Jacksdale with
a Nottingham Victoria–Pinxton local.
Note the Great Northern somersault
signal. Jacksdale station would close on
7 January 1963, No 43082 surviving,
latterly at Langwith shed, until
November 1965. *T. G. Hepburn /
Rail Archive Stephenson*

The Power of the
LMS 2-6-0s

Gavin Morrison

OPC

An imprint of
Ian Allan Publishing

Contents

First published 2005

ISBN (10) 0 86093 595 7
ISBN (13) 978 0 86093 595 7

Published by Ian Allan Publishing

an imprint of Ian Allan Publishing Ltd, Hersham, Surrey KT12 4RG
Printed in England by Ian Allan Printing Ltd, Hersham, Surrey KT12 4RG

Code: 0511/A3

Visit the Ian Allan Publishing website at www.ianallanpublishing.com

Introduction

The 'Power' series of books with which I have been involved over the last 28 years has generally featured one class of locomotive, or very similar classes. This volume, featuring the LMS Moguls, deals with widely differing locomotives built between 1926 and 1947. Embracing smaller locomotives with lighter axle loads, it has also allowed me to illustrate lines barred to the larger locomotives covered previously.

The origin of the name 'Mogul' is unknown. The 2-6-0 wheel arrangement was first used by the Midland Railway in 1899 on some American-built locomotives, although it had first appeared in this country back in 1878 on the Great Eastern Railway.

In the mid-1920s the LMS was in urgent need of a powerful mixed-traffic design. Prior to the Grouping in 1923 the Caledonian Railway had designed a 2-6-0 which the Locomotive Department of the newly formed LMS thought might be the answer, until it was discovered that such a locomotive would be out of gauge for many lines on the LMS network. The Chief Mechanical Engineers from the constituent companies of the LMS formed a committee to discuss a design; perhaps not surprisingly they could not agree, but they did instruct Chief Draughtsman J. R. Billington to go back to Horwich Works and design a suitable locomotive.

Under the direction of CME George Hughes and using the Caledonian design as a basis, Billington came up with a locomotive incorporating a higher level of superheating and higher boiler pressure, with a driving-wheel diameter of 5ft 6in and large (21x26in) angled cylinders, this last feature giving rise to the 'Crab' nickname by which the type would become known. Although the class is usually attributed to Sir Henry Fowler he had little to do with the design, which had been completed before he took over as CME in 1925, but he did insist that the locomotives be attached to standard 3,500gal tenders of Midland Railway design; these were narrower than the locomotives themselves, giving a rather odd appearance from certain angles, but were to remain with the locomotives throughout their lives, although their water capacity would turn out to be rather small for the work the locomotives were called upon to perform.

Some 245 locomotives were constructed, and in their early years they were spread all over the LMS from the Highland lines to the Somerset & Dorset and most places in between. The class proved extremely popular with crews, especially in Scotland, being good steamers and extremely powerful, albeit rather wild-riding at speed, and it soon became clear that they were suitable for parcels and passenger work as well as freight.

Title page:
A fine study of LMS No 2971, new in 1934 (as No 13271), one of a batch of 40 Moguls built under the ægis of William Stanier. *T.G. Hepburn / Rail Archive Stephenson*

Right:
The first 100 Hughes/Fowler 'Crab' 2-6-0s were painted in crimson lake, which must have looked superb. Here No 13065 is pictured passing London Road Junction as it leaves Nottingham with an excursion for St Pancras in the late 1920s. Renumbered as 2765 in 1934 and again by BR as 42765, this locomotive was to remain in service until December 1966. Rescued from Barry scrapyard in April 1978, it has since been returned to working order on the East Lancashire Railway.
T. G. Hepburn / Rail Archive Stephenson

It is testimony to the soundness of the design that they carried on for around 40 years without modification. An exception concerned five examples fitted in 1931 with Lentz rotary-poppet valvegear, which was replaced in 1952/3 with Reidinger rotary-cam valvegear, but these modifications showed little or no benefit over the standard design, although the five locomotives retained the modifications until withdrawn. From the mid-1930s the class was ousted from main-line duties by the Stanier Class 5s, but when called upon could stand in for the 'Black Fives' and were just as powerful, if not as fast. They continued in service until January 1967 on all manner of duties, being particularly popular in the Ayr district until steam finished in Scotland in October 1966. They were an excellent class, and fortunately three examples survive in preservation.

In the early 1930s the LMS identified a need for further Moguls. William Stanier, who by this time had taken over as CME, was fully aware that what it really needed was some high-powered express engines. To this end he decided to design his own Mogul, with Churchward-style taper boiler, as a way of getting Crewe and Derby used to this feature, which he believed superior to the parallel boiler.

The first of the class emerged from Crewe Works in October 1933 and quickly entered service. All 40 locomotives were attached to the narrow Fowler tenders, which suited them better than they did the 'Crabs'. The Stanier locomotives were known in some circles as 'Camels', on account of the humps on the boiler.

Spending nearly all their time at the Western Division sheds of the LMS (albeit on a wide variety of duties, the Stanier Moguls seemed always to be in the background. They were seldom seen on the Settle–Carlisle line, and workings north of the border were virtually unknown other than in 1934, when Nos 13248 and 13251 were used on Carlisle–Glasgow stopping trains and No 13254 worked some Glasgow–Aberdeen expresses. Having few regular diagrams, they were difficult to photograph; in latter years the North Wales coast in summer was usually a good bet for passenger workings, but it was a very hit-and-miss affair. The class was seldom used on railtours, not featuring in any of the 174 tours (some as joint ventures) organised by the Railway Correspondence & Travel Society (RCTS).

Withdrawals commenced in 1963, the last example surviving until July 1966. Fortunately No 42968 has been preserved and has put in performances which must have surprised those who knew or drove these engines in their working days; in preservation it has run with a Stanier tender, but this writer prefers it with the earlier Fowler design.

Right:
In 1934 the power rating for the Stanier 2-6-0s was altered from 4F to 5P4F, in recognition of their capabilities when hauling passenger trains. In this early view of No 13268 the original classification is just discernible above the side windows; unfortunately neither the precise date nor the location are recorded.
Rail Archive Stephenson

Left:
The first of H. G. Ivatt's Class 4 Moguls, No 43000, on shed at its home depot of Carlisle Canal on 6 April 1963, two months before that shed closed. The locomotive would be withdrawn in September 1967 from North Blyth after nearly 20 years in service. *Gavin Morrison*

No new LMS Moguls were designed until 1946/7, when Ivatt's '2MTs' and '4MTs' (known initially as '2Fs' and '4Fs' respectively) appeared on the scene. In terms of design philosophy these were very different from anything which had run previously in this country and no doubt came as a considerable shock to most engineers.

Ivatt realised that the postwar years on the railways were going to be very different from the pre-1938 era, when labour costs had been relatively low and maintenance standards and coal quality high, so he based his new designs on the American principle whereby everything should be accessible and simple, to keep maintenance to a minimum. In this he certainly succeeded (albeit at the expense of looks), his Moguls being fitted with many features such as self-cleaning smokeboxes, rocking gates, self-emptying ashpans, side-window cabs and tender cabs, which were much appreciated by the crews and staff. Both classes were fast and economical, but both suffered with rather poor steaming, especially the '4MTs' which were fitted with a (very large) double chimney; the three '4MTs' sent to the Somerset & Dorset line were found to be badly wanting on the steep gradients and were soon transferred away.

With the Nationalisation of the 'Big Four' main-line railway companies only 20 '2MTs' and just three '4MTs' actually entered traffic in LMS days, but production of both types would continue under BR, the former eventually numbering 128, the latter 162.

Designed to replace the large number of life-expired LMS 4-4-0s and 0-6-0s on secondary duties, the Ivatt Moguls would also be used in BR days to replace the likes of ex-GWR 'Dean Goods' and Collett 0-6-0s, especially on Cambrian and Mid-Wales lines.

Problems with draughting prompted Derby and Swindon works to conduct experiments involving rather ugly stovepipe chimneys and other designs, many of which are illustrated in this book. The problems solved, the Ivatt Moguls were transformed into free-steaming, fast-running and smooth-riding locomotives, many lasting until the end of steam on BR (and many of their features being incorporated into the BR Standard designs). The 'Power' series title might be considered somewhat inappropriate in relation to a '2MT' locomotive, so it is worth mentioning that in tests following modification at Swindon No 46413 was diagrammed to haul a 15-coach 455-ton test train up a 1-in-300 gradient, which it achieved at up to 40mph at 42% cut-off — some performance for such a small engine.

The 14-ton axle-load of the '2MTs' gave them a very wide route availability. Furthermore, they were quite happy at 60mph (I once travelled at 73mph on a two-coach train between Keighley and Skipton) and would run up 100,000 miles plus between overhauls. The same applied to the '4MTs', speeds of 80mph being not unknown.

From the early 1960s line closures and the introduction of diesels saw the Ivatt 2-6-0s ousted from many of the duties for which they were designed, so most achieved only 15-20 years of service. Fortunately examples of both classes have been preserved.

Left:
Ivatt Class 2 No 46443 when just over three years old, at Nottingham Midland on 13 May 1953. Allocated for many years to Derby shed, it would be withdrawn from Newton Heath shed, Manchester, in March 1967, thereafter passing into preservation on the Severn Valley Railway. *J. P. Wilson / Rail Archive Stephenson*

Left:
The first NCC Mogul, No 90
(later to be named *Duke of Abercorn*)
as turned out by Derby Works
in LMS maroon in 1933.
Ian Allan Library

For the sake of completeness, it is perhaps worth mentioning that 15 further 2-6-0s were built for use in Northern Ireland by the Northern Counties Committee (NCC), which railway was a subsidiary of the LMS (and, before that, the Midland Railway). The locomotives in question constituted NCC Class W and were built in two batches, the first four emerging from Derby Works in 1933, the remainder being assembled by the NCC at Belfast during the period 1934-42. Built to Northern Ireland's 5ft 3in gauge, they otherwise showed a marked similarity to locomotive designs turned out by Derby in the early 1930s. However, with their 6ft driving wheels they were more suited to passenger work than mixed traffic, being intended for use on the NCC's principal expresses. In 1948, when the LMS was nationalised, all 15 locomotives were taken into stock by the newly created Railway Executive (Northern Counties Committee), before passing in 1949 to the Ulster Transport Authority (UTA). The last examples remained in service until 1965, but sadly none survived to be preserved.

As always I should like to thank all the photographers whose work appears in this book, and to the authors of the books and magazine articles (listed in the Bibliography) from which I have obtained technical information; finally I should like to express my gratitude to the volunteers working on those preserved lines that keep examples of LMS 2-6-0s running for everybody to enjoy.

Gavin Morrison
Mirfield
September 2005

Bibliography
Fowler Locomotives by Brian Haresnape (Ian Allan, 1972)
Stanier Locomotives by Brian Haresnape (Ian Allan, 1970)
Ivatt and Riddles Locomotives by Brian Haresnape
 (Ian Allan, 1977)
Locomotives Illustrated Nos 22 and 72
 (Ian Allan, 1980 and 1990)

Left:
By now in UTA ownership,
one of the later NCC Moguls,
No 100 *Queen Elizabeth,* is seen
near Whiteabbey at the head of a
Belfast–Portrush express in July 1955.
Note the Stanier-style tender.
For a short period, in 1947/8,
this locomotive, along with No 101,
ran as an oil-burner. *Nigel Craig*

Hughes/Fowler Locomotives

Left:
A fine portrait of 'Crab' No 13085 in the unlined crimson lake applied to the first 100 members of the class. Pictured at Crewe South shed, probably in the late 1920s, it would be withdrawn in November 1963 after just over 36 years of service. *T. G. Hepburn / Rail Archive Stephenson*

Variations and Liveries

Left:
A picture of Hughes/Fowler 'Crab' No 13183 taken between June 1930, when it was built, and 1934, when it received its second LMS number (2883). As BR No 42883 this locomotive would be withdrawn in December 1962 after spending several years allocated to Carlisle Kingmoor shed. *Ian Allan Library*

Left:
A few members of the class that received works overhauls just after nationalisation of the railways in 1948 received this livery, with the number prefixed by the letter 'M'. No 2923 is shown thus in unlined black, with full 'BRITISH RAILWAYS' lettering on the tender. *Ian Allan Library*

Right:
Following nationalisation most of the 'Crabs' received their new five-digit numbers but retained 'L M S' tender lettering until they visited works for a major overhaul. Displaying this combination while allocated to Saltley shed, No 42784 would survive until December 1962. *Ian Allan Library*

Below:
In lined black with 'BRITISH RAILWAYS' lettering on the tender, Derby-allocated No 42872 is seen in charge of an express at an unidentified location *c*1949. This locomotive would survive until December 1963. *C. Ord / Rail Archive Stephenson*

Left:
Apparently just released from St Rollox Works at Glasgow, No 42809 stands on shed at Balornock (65B) in July 1955. The livery features the early style of lion-and-wheel emblem but incorporates larger-than-normal cabside numbers, as applied to locomotives overhauled at St Rollox and Springburn. The 67C shedplate indicates that No 42809 was allocated to Ayr, as were many other members of the class. This example would remain in service until in December 1962. *Ian Allan Library*

Left:
The only time one usually saw a clean Carlisle Kingmoor 'Crab' was when it was newly ex works. No 42882 looks immaculate at its home shed on 14 June 1959 after returning from St Rollox Works with later style of lion-and-wheel emblem. *Gavin Morrison*

Below left:
During a works visit sometime after September 1953 No 42770 had its original tender exchanged for this flush-sided example, with the lining following the top edge; note also the large emblem. Having spent many years postwar allocated to Hellifield and Manningham sheds, being seen at the latter in very clean condition on 25 January 1959, this locomotive would be withdrawn in November 1963. *Gavin Morrison*

Below:
Some measure of the success of the Horwich 2-6-0 design can be gained from the fact that, of 245 locomotives built, only five underwent significant modification. These were Nos 13118/22/4/5/8, which between December 1931 and February 1932 received Lentz rotary cam poppet valvegear. This official picture of No 13124 clearly shows the 5P4F classification on the cabside. Latterly numbered 42824, this locomotive would remain in service until July 1962. *Ian Allan Library*

Right:
Another of the Lentz poppet-valve locomotives, No 2822 (originally 13122), at an unidentified location, probably in the late 1930s. This example would survive until June 1962. *Ian Allan Library*

Below:
A 1939 picture of Lentz poppet-valve No 2824 near Churchdown on a working from Gloucester to Lowestoft, consisting of a wide variety of coaches. *Ian Allan Library*

Right:
Apparently the revised valvegear showed no advantages over the standard Walschaerts gearing and some 20 years later (between April 1952 and January 1954) was replaced on all five locomotives by the Reidinger version. Allocated to Saltley shed Birmingham, No 42818 is shown awaiting this modification at Horwich Works on 20 September 1953. This locomotive would be the first of the quintet to be withdrawn, in May 1962, the other four following by July of that year. *Gavin Morrison*

Left:
The LMS renumbering scheme was introduced in 1934, but on 21 July 1935 what was by now officially No 2934 was still carrying its original number (13234) as it headed a van train along the West Coast main line at Kilburn. Versatile locomotives, the 'Crabs' were happy on almost any type of train, but it got rather rough on the footplate over the 50mph mark.
E. R. Wethersett

Below:
A 'Crab' on express-passenger work. No 2760 heads a Sheffield–St Pancras train near Elstree on 5 June 1937. New in June 1927 as No 13060, this locomotive would last until August 1964, its final allocation being Gorton, near Manchester.
E. R. Wethersett

Above:
A superb picture of No 13127 getting away from Nottingham in charge of an up excursion *c*1931, with no fewer than 13 coaches behind the tender. Twice renumbered (by the LMS as 2827 and by BR as 42827), it would be withdrawn in August 1965. *T. G. Hepburn / Rail Archive Stephenson*

Below:
In its crimson-lake livery No 13035 must have made a superb sight passing Kenton at the head of the 7pm Class D down goods on a fine summer's evening in 1927. Latterly numbered 42735, it was to survive until November 1963. *F. R. Hebron / Rail Archive Stephenson*

Above:
Burton-upon-Trent-allocated
No 42855 approaches Luton with a
down train of empties, heading for its
home town. The locomotive had
entered service in March 1930 and
would survive until September 1964.
*S. Summerson / Rail Archive
Stephenson*

Right:
In steam days Birmingham New Street
station was a very atmospheric
location for photography. Here the
light catches No 42897 as it prepares
to leave with the 6.25pm stopping
train to Derby on 17 September
1958. The locomotive would achieve
almost 34 years of service, surviving
until April 1964. *M. Mensing*

Left:
No 42823, allocated to Nottingham Midland shed, makes a fine sight departing Bulwell Market with a rake of Gresley coaches forming an excursion to Skegness on 22 August 1959. The ex-Midland Railway station would close to passengers with effect from 12 October 1964, having survived the 'Crab' by just three months. *T. G. Hepburn / Rail Archive Stephenson*

Above:
Another 'Crab' allocated to Nottingham Midland was No 42855, shown passing Basford Sidings signalbox with the 11.24am Mablethorpe–Radford, which would have travelled via Lincoln and Mansfield Town, on 27 July 1963. Transferred to Bury, it would be withdrawn in September 1964. *T. G. Hepburn / Rail Archive Stephenson*

Above:
Heaton Norris, at the north end of the viaduct over Stockport, was a fine photographic location with impressive gantries and large Victorian warehouses. No 42858, allocated to Manchester Longsight between 1950 and 1959, heads for Manchester London Road (now Piccadilly) with a down express in the 1950s. This locomotive would survive until April 1964. *J. Davenport / N. Stead collection*

Below:
No 42838 emerges from the tunnel at the east end of Blackburn station with an empty-stock working on 8 September 1962, its 24B shedplate indicating allocation to Rose Grove. The locomotive would be withdrawn only six months after this picture was taken, in March 1963. *N. Stead collection*

Left:
The 'Crabs' were well capable of the hard work necessary to haul trains over the difficult Midland main line through the Peak District. Here we see No 42769 climbing away from Chee Tor Tunnels, near Millers Dale, with an excursion on 2 April 1956. This locomotive would put in 36½ years of service, finally being withdrawn in February 1964.
M. Mensing

Left:
Another view at Chee Tor Tunnels, again on 2 April 1956, this time showing Burton-upon-Trent's No 42826 in charge of an eight-coach excursion. Subsequently transferred to Stockport Edgley shed, it would be withdrawn in September 1964.
M. Mensing

Above right:
The first of two pictures featuring locomotives fitted with Reidinger rotary-cam poppet valvegear. No 42825 appears to be going well with its nine-coach Manchester Central–St Pancras relief express as it approaches Chinley Junction, on the long (17-mile) climb — mainly at 1 in 90 — from Cheadle Heath to Peak Forest at 4.45pm on 16 July 1955. No 42825 would be withdrawn in June 1962, the other locomotives similarly equipped succumbing at around the same time. *T. Lewis*

Right:
No 42818, allocated to Burton-upon-Trent, is in fine external condition as it heads a coal train near Disley Tunnel, bound for Gowhole sidings on 30 August 1958. It would nevertheless be the first of the Reidinger locomotives to be withdrawn, in May 1962. *K. Field / Rail Archive Stephenson*

Left:
The 'Crabs' were frequently seen along the North Wales coast on summer extras, although (postwar, at least) they were not allocated to any of the local sheds. No 42926 is seen west of Rhyl with the 5.35pm Llandudno–Crewe on 23 August 1959, at which time it was a Crewe South engine. It would be withdrawn in October 1964, by then reallocated to Rose Grove. *M. Mensing*

Below:
No 42727 had been well cleaned to work an SLS special along the North Wales coast and around the Wirral on 27 March 1966, being shown leaving Llandudno Junction at the start of its journey back to Birmingham.
No 42727 would be the penultimate member of the class to remain in traffic, being withdrawn in January 1967 shortly before No 42942, the very last. *Brian Stephenson*

Above:
For many years the 'Crabs' were almost daily visitors to the Calder Valley main line. Although employed on a wide variety of workings, they were generally rostered for stopping trains; climbing towards Summit Tunnel, No 42864 is seen crossing Gauxholme Viaduct, a couple of miles from Todmorden, with a Burnley–Manchester train which would have travelled via Copy Pit. Regrettably this fine picture is undated, but judging by the coaches it must have been taken in the early 1950s. The locomotive would be one of the first three of its type to be withdrawn, in July 1961.
K. Field / Rail Archive Stephenson

Right:
Pictured heading a Bradford Exchange–Manchester Victoria express in the early 1950s, No 42842 has just emerged from the very short Rochdale Road Tunnel, encountered immediately after the 2,885yd-long Summit Tunnel on the Lancashire side. The locomotive would end its days at Fleetwood shed in June 1964.
K. Field / Rail Archive Stephenson

Above:
No 42841 eases out of the one-time Lancashire & Yorkshire side of Preston station with a Fleetwood–Salford fish train. Fleetwood shed had an allocation of 'Crabs' for many years, fish trains being one of their principal duties. First allocated there in 1950, No 42841 would still be on strength in 1964, finally being withdrawn in March 1965. *D. T. Greenwood / Rail Archive Stephenson*

Left:
Today only the two lines behind the station board remain, but back in 1960, when this photograph was taken, Diggle was a much busier centre. No 42845 heads east with a Sunday Stockport–Bradford Exchange (very) mixed van train. It is travelling on the original 1849 line and is just about to enter one of the single-bore Standedge tunnels, which were 5,342yd long; that which No 42845 is about to enter was known as the Nicholson Tunnel after its engineer, Thomas Nicholson. *K. Field / Rail Archive Stephenson*

On a fine spring evening (13 May 1961) one of Newton Heath's allocation of 'Crabs', No 42726, puts up an impressive exhaust as it approaches Ais Gill Summit (1,169ft) with a freight for Lancashire. For many years the class would be a frequent sight on freight over the Settle–Carlisle line, as Carlisle Kingmoor shed had a sizeable allocation, as did Leeds Holbeck and Newton Heath, Manchester. Having entered service in November 1927 as LMS No 13026, this example would be withdrawn in October 1962. *Gavin Morrison*

Right:
One of Crewe South's 'Crabs', No 42885, overfills its tender on Dillicar troughs, just to the south of Tebay station, as it heads an up freight through the Lune Gorge. This locomotive would remain in service until December 1963.
W. J. V. Anderson / Rail Archive Stephenson

On the Eastern and North Eastern Regions

Below:
Saltley-allocated No 42823 passes Firsby, Lincolnshire, with a special from the London Midland Region to Skegness on 23 August 1959. Note the ex-Great Northern somersault signals. The locomotive had entered service in October 1929 as LMS No 13123 and would be withdrawn in July 1964. *N. Stead collection*

Above:
The 'Crabs' were frequent visitors to the Yorkshire and Lincolnshire seaside resorts in the summer months. Here, devoid of shedplate, No 42754 heads special M286 into Scarborough from Sheffield, having travelled via Bridlington. The picture is undated but must have been taken in the early 1950s, as the coaches are still in carmine-and-cream livery. The locomotive would survive until November 1964. *K. Hoole / N. Stead collection*

Below:
Allocated to Burton-upon-Trent, No 42799 heads away from Cleethorpes on the return leg of an excursion from Belper. Note the fairground, complete with 'big dipper', in the background. No 42799 would last until January 1965. *N. Stead collection*

Left:
Wakefield's No 42862 pulls away from Bridlington station, heading south towards Beverley on the return journey of an excursion from Bradford Exchange on 13 June 1959. This locomotive would be withdrawn in December 1962, after more than 32 years' service. *N. Stead collection*

Below left:
Wakefield's No 42863 passes the east end of Brighouse yard, on the Calder Valley main line, with the 10.30am Liverpool Exchange–Newcastle express on 18 June 1959. It had obviously been pressed into service to cover for a failure, as the regular motive power for this working was one of Liverpool Bank Hall's three 'Jubilees' — *Mars, Dauntless* or *Glorious* — or its unnamed, unrebuilt 'Patriot', No 45517. The 'Crab' would last until August 1966. *Gavin Morrison*

Bottom left:
Newton Heath-allocated No 42725 leaves Greetland bound for Manchester Victoria via the Calder Valley main line with a stopping train on the evening of 14 July 1959. The line on the far left is headed for Halifax. Greetland station would close with effect from 10 September 1962, No 42725 surviving it by two years, until October 1964. *Gavin Morrison*

Above right:
Another of Wakefield's 'Crabs', No 42862, approaches Low Moor with an excursion from Bradford Exchange to Blackpool on 8 October 1961, by which time it had barely a year's service ahead of it. *Gavin Morrison*

Right:
In steam days the (then) daily Heaton–Red Bank empty vans was always double-headed over the Pennines and produced a wide variety of locomotive combinations. On 23 July 1956 two Newton Heath engines — 'Crab' No 42701 and Stanier 'Black Five' No 45284 — were in charge, being pictured on Luddendenfoot water troughs on their way up the valley towards Hebden Bridge. No 42701 was to put in more than 38 years of service, finally being withdrawn in December 1964. *Gavin Morrison*

Left:
No 42930 heads an up coal train past Marsden, near the end of the long climb from Heaton Lodge Junction towards the single-bore Nelson Tunnel through the Pennines at Standedge, which opened in 1871. The fireman appears to have the fire well under control judging by the lack of exhaust, which would undoubtedly make the 5,342yd journey through the tunnel more pleasant. The '9A' shedplate denotes allocation to Longsight shed, where this locomotive was based between 1950 and 1959. *K. Field / Rail Archive Stephenson*

Left:
The last of the 'Crabs' to remain in service was No 42942, at Birkenhead shed. On 8 October 1966 this locomotive hauled the LCGB's 'Crab Commemorative' railtour, which ran via the Calder Valley main line and then via Halifax, Low Moor, down the Spen Valley line to Thornhill and Wakefield, where it handed over to a 'WD' 2-8-0 for the run to Goole. In this view the train has just left Beacon Hill Tunnel and is approaching Hipperholme, between Halifax and Low Moor. Note the letters 'L M' visible on the tender. No 42942's career would finally draw to a close in January 1967. *Gavin Morrison*

Above right:
Another of Wakefield's 'Crabs' out and about on excursion duties. No 42863 is pictured rounding the sharp curve past Marsden prior to entering the single-bore Nelson Tunnel at Standedge with a train from the West Riding to Blackpool Illuminations on 26 September 1959. *Gavin Morrison*

Right:
Springwood Junction signal box, just to the west of Huddersfield, must have been a dirty place to work, being situated in a deep 'hole' between two tunnels. It is also the point at which the Penistone line branches off. Here we see No 42774, allocated to Leeds Holbeck, hard at work on the 1-in-105 gradient at the head of an excursion on 20 October 1953. This locomotive would be withdrawn in November 1963. *K. Field / Rail Archive Stephenson*

Right:
This superb picture shows 'Crab' No 13016 in its original crimson livery at the entrance to the tunnel at the west end of Huddersfield station, shortly after entering service in May 1927. The train is the Bradford Exchange–Marylebone express, which in later years would be known as the 'South Yorkshireman'. The locomotive was most likely allocated to Low Moor shed at Bradford and would probably have worked as far as Sheffield Victoria. Latterly as BR No 42706, it would be in service for 38 years, until April 1965. *P. F. Cooke / Rail Archive Stephenson*

Right:
The Midland main line north of Leeds was for many years well used by the 'Crabs', on local passenger and freight. Lancaster shed provided the locomotives for most of the passenger workings and had a small but stable allocation for more than 10 years. They arrived c1950, chiefly to replace LMS Compounds, and stayed until replaced c1962 by unrebuilt 'Patriots', which lasted only a short time before Stanier Class 5s and ultimately diesel locomotives took over. On 31 July 1961 — long before a platform was opened on the direct line to Leeds at Shipley — 'Crab' No 42851 of Lancaster shed negotiates the sharp curve with an up local train. This locomotive would continue in service until May 1964. *Gavin Morrison*

Below right:
Another view taken on the Shipley curve, this time featuring No 42778 heading an up train of empty coal wagons back to the South Yorkshire coalfield of on 23 May 1963. The locomotive would be withdrawn from Bolton shed in April 1965. *Gavin Morrison*

Above:
Stockport-allocated 'Crab' No 42848 passes Mirfield shed, playing host to a 'WD' 2-8-0 and a locally based Fowler 2-6-4T, at the head of a Leeds–Stockport stopping train on the afternoon of 10 June 1960. This location has been a favourite for local enthusiasts over the years, although just three lines now remain and the mill chimneys have gone. No 42848 would continue in service until March 1965. *Gavin Morrison*

Left:
Superpower for a Leeds–Manchester local approaching the bridge leading to Mirfield golf course, between Thornhill Junction and Mirfield, No 42817 piloting Farnley Junction 'Jubilee' No 45695 *Minotaur*. The picture is undated but was probably taken after September 1952, when the 'Jubilee' was transferred from Liverpool Bank Hall; both locomotives still have the early lion-and-wheel emblem. Thornhill power station in the background has long since gone as have the mill chimneys. No 42817 would remain in service until April 1965, thereby surviving the 'Jubilee' by almost a year. *K. Field / Rail Archive Stephenson*

Left:
Approximately halfway between Keighley and Bingley, Kingmoor-allocated 'Crab' No 42830 approaches Marley Junction with an up fitted freight on 16 May 1962. Allocated to Carlisle Kingmoor for many years postwar, this locomotive would be withdrawn in November 1962 after more than 32 years in service.
Gavin Morrison

Below left:
On 13 April 1962 No 42795 was employed on humble duties, being seen passing Marley Junction, between Keighley and Bingley, with a weed-killer train. This appears to be much less sophisticated than its modern equivalent, but at least the chemicals really killed the weeds! No 42795 would be one of the last of the class to be withdrawn, in November 1966.
Gavin Morrison

Top right:
No 42928 was first allocated to Lancaster shed in 1950 and was still based there in the early 1960s, being a regular performer on Morecambe–Leeds passenger workings and parcels trains. In the first of three photographs featuring it on this route, the locomotive is seen approaching Hellifield with an up local on 14 October 1961.
Gavin Morrison

Above right:
No 42928 passes Calverley & Rodley with a train heading south for Leeds on 27 February 1960. The carriages seen on the right of the picture were a feature for many years, being patched up and used on summer extras for only a few days each year. The station itself would close with effect from 20 March 1965, and today only two tracks remain at this location.
Gavin Morrison

Right:
A last look at No 42928, captured here between Wortley Junction and Whitehall Junction as it approaches Leeds City with a local train from Morecambe on 1 May 1962. The locomotive would be withdrawn in September 1965. *Gavin Morrison*

A Morecambe–Leeds express approaches Bingley from the north on 10 May 1962 behind 'Crab' No 42931, which spent its last years at Lancaster before being withdrawn in September 1964. *Gavin Morrison*

Left:
No 42905 heads an up freight through the Aire Valley as it approaches Connonley station, a few miles south of Skipton, on 8 August 1962. A Kingmoor locomotive for much of its postwar career, it would end its days at Bury, in July 1965. *Gavin Morrison*

Right:
A Lancaster locomotive since 1950, No 42895 pulls away from Hellifield with a stopping train from Leeds to Morecambe on 4 November 1961. It would be withdrawn in January 1963. *Gavin Morrison*

Right:
The 'Crabs' constituted the principal motive power on express-passenger workings over the Highland main line from around 1928 until ousted from the mid-1930s by the Stanier Class 5s. This superb picture shows Nos 13103 and 13101 approaching Hermitage Tunnel, north of Dunkeld, at the head of the 3.45pm Inverness–Glasgow Buchanan Street in the early 1930s. Both locomotives would remain allocated to Scotland, ending their respective careers in the Ayrshire coalfield in November and June 1966.
F. R. Hebron / Rail Archive Stephenson

Below:
In Ayrshire the 'Crabs' were normally to be seen on coal trains, but they were also used for piloting specials, especially on the steep gradients south of Ayr. On 22 June 1962 No 42910 was photographed assisting Stanier 'Black Five' No 45486 with a schools excursion from Dalmellington to Ardrossan, the combination being seen passing Dalrymple Junction. Both locomotives were allocated to Ayr. No 42910 would be withdrawn in November 1963. *D. Cross*

On the Scottish Region

Above:
Unfortunately this picture is undated, but judging by the snowfall it may well have been taken during the winter of 1962/3. Having left the Ayr–Stranraer main line at Dalrymple Junction, Ayr's No 42916 returns empty coal wagons to Waterside Colliery. This locomotive would continue in service around Ayr until June 1965. *D. Cross*

Below:
In charge of an empty-stock train from Ayr to Stranraer, Stanier Class 5MT No 44769 of Crewe receives assistance from local 'Crab' No 42914, the combination being seen passing Dalrymple Junction on its journey south. No 42914 would remain in service until December 1963, the 'Black Fives until July 1965. *D. Cross*

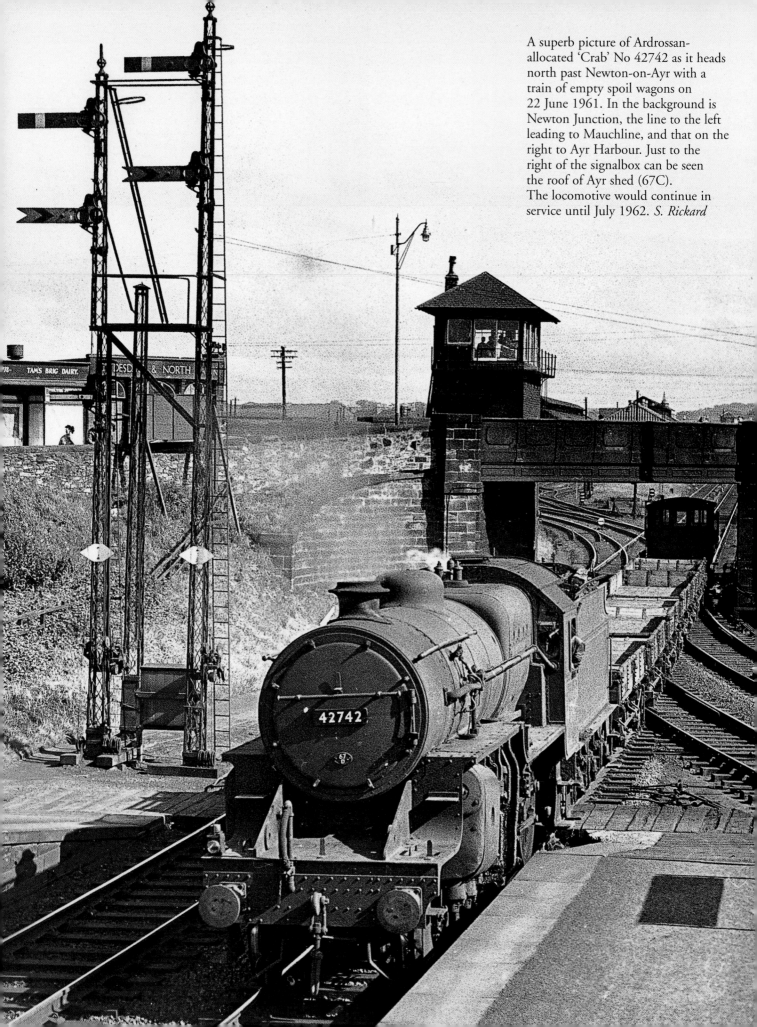

A superb picture of Ardrossan-allocated 'Crab' No 42742 as it heads north past Newton-on-Ayr with a train of empty spoil wagons on 22 June 1961. In the background is Newton Junction, the line to the left leading to Mauchline, and that on the right to Ayr Harbour. Just to the right of the signalbox can be seen the roof of Ayr shed (67C). The locomotive would continue in service until July 1962. *S. Rickard*

Above:
In LMS black livery, No 2880 has just crossed Ligg Viaduct, between Barrhill and Pinmore Summit (394ft), with a train from Stranraer to Glasgow St Enoch in 1936. Renumbered 42880 in BR days, this locomotive would survive until November 1964. *F. R. Hebron / Rail Archive Stephenson*

Below:
The National Coal Board's preparation plant at Waterside had its own Barclay 0-6-0 saddle tank for shunting duties, seen here in the mid-1960s as No 42801 of Ayr shed passes with the morning Dalmellington–Ayr goods. The 'Crab' would be withdrawn in June 1966. *D. Cross*

Left:
The 'Crabs' were considered by
crews working in the Ayrshire
coalfield to be fine locomotives,
not only for their ability to climb
stiff gradients but also (and even
more importantly) for their braking
capabilities on the way down.
Seen passing Mossblown Junction,
on the outskirts of Ayr, No 42803
brings a loaded coal train from
Killoch Pit down to Ayr Harbour
on 8 May 1963. Its career would
end in November 1966. *D. Cross*

Below left:
Dumfries had a small allocation
of 'Crabs', used mainly on the line
to Stranraer. Here No 42918 stands
on the turntable at its home shed.
A Dumfries locomotive from 1950,
it would remain allocated there until
withdrawal in December 1962.
*T. G. Hepburn / Rail Archive
Stephenson*

Above right:
In the first of two pictures featuring 'Crabs' on the Dumfries–Stranraer line, No 42914 pulls away from Newton Stewart,
heading east downhill to Palnure, before tackling 6½ miles at 1 in 80 to the summit at Gatehouse of Fleet on 15 July 1963.
It would be withdrawn five months later. *M. Mensing*

Below:
Having just shunted a wagon into the sidings at Creetown, No 42919 prepares to depart westwards with a pick-up goods
from Castle Douglas to Stranraer, also on 15 July 1963. Creetown station would close from 14 June 1965, the 'Crab'
remaining in service until October 1966. *M. Mensing*

Above:
The exhaust from a banking locomotive is just discernible above the signalbox as Grangemouth's No 42803, apparently in ex-works condition, pulls away from Beattock station with a down freight on 4 July 1958. Just visible on shed to the right of the signalbox are two Caledonian 0-4-4Ts. No 42803 would be withdrawn in November 1966 from the Ayr area. *K. L. Cook / Rail Archive Stephenson*

Left:
Having just passed Greskine distant signal, Carlisle Kingmoor-allocated No 42793 storms the 1-in-75 gradient of Beattock Bank (blowing off at the same time!), with a Fairburn 2-6-4T giving a helping hand at the rear, on Easter Sunday (21 April) 1957. The 'Crab' would remain at work until December 1964, ending its days at Stockport Edgeley. *W. J. V. Anderson / Rail Archive Stephenson*

Stanier Locomotives

Right:
The first of the Stanier Class 4 2-6-0s, No 13245, emerges from the erecting shops at Crewe on 21 October 1933. Stanier's design looked very different from the Hughes/Fowler 'Crab' but was still attached to a Fowler tender which was narrower than the locomotive. In an attempt to please Stanier, who had begun his career on the Great Western Railway, Horwich Works incorporated a GWR 'coffee-pot' safety-valve casing, as seen here; however, this apparently met with the designer's disapproval, and it was swiftly removed. Whether the engine ever worked a train in this condition is not known. *Ian Allan Library*

Right:
Now with dome-shaped casing incorporating the safety valves, No 13245 stands on shed at Crewe South on 7 April 1934 in LMS black livery. Note the '4F' classification above the cab windows. *T. G. Hepburn / Rail Archive Stephenson*

Variations and Liveries

Right:
New as Nos 13245-84, the Stanier Moguls were renumbered by the LMS in 1934 as 2945-84 and again by BR as 42945-84. Seen on shed at Derby on 10 July 1948, six months after nationalisation, No 42954 has had its new number applied but still proclaims 'L M S' on its tender. The locomotive shows the type of boiler fitted to the first 10 of the class, which was modified for remaining 30. *T. G. Hepburn / Rail Archive Stephenson*

Above:
Clearly showing the safety valve in the dome casing, No 2951 passes Bushey water troughs with an up goods on 20 June 1936. When new the class was allocated to all four operating divisions of the LMS. Renumbered 42951 in BR days, this locomotive would be withdrawn in March 1966 after 35 years of service. *E. R. Wethersett*

Below:
Although officially renumbered the previous year No 13271 still retained its original identity when photographed passing Brock water troughs with an up meat train in 1935. Fitted with the later type of boiler, with safety valve above the firebox, the locomotive would be withdrawn in December 1964. *F. R. Hebron / Rail Archive Stephenson*

Right:
Looking very smart in lined BR black livery, following an overhaul at Horwich Works, No 42959 stands on shed at Bolton in July 1949. The locomotive is fitted with the later type of boiler, with safety valve above the firebox. *Ian Allan Library*

Right:
Visiting Leeds on trains from across the Pennines, the Stanier Moguls were seen frequently at Farnley Junction shed but not at Holbeck. Mold Junction's No 42969, in BR lined black with early lion-and-wheel emblem on the tender, was thus an unusual visitor to the latter on 21 April 1961. *Gavin Morrison*

Right:
Low Moor shed, near Bradford, was another which seldom saw the class, but on the evening of 1 October 1963 No 42982 was present, again in BR lined black but with the later style of lion-and-wheel emblem. *Gavin Morrison*

On the London Midland Region

Below:
Showing an express headcode, No 42984 passes Watery Lane signalbox (near Tipton) with the 8.10pm Birmingham New Street–Chester on 7 July 1959, at which time it was allocated to Crewe South shed.
M. Mensing

Left:
Its 21D shedplate revealing it to be an Aston engine, No 42956 carries out shunting duties at Stechford on 5 June 1961. This locomotive would be withdrawn in September 1964.
M. Mensing

Above:
The North Wales Coast line was probably one of the best for seeing the class at work over the years. Here Mold Junction's No 42971 arrives at Llandudno Junction with an up freight, probably in the late 1950s. The locomotive would be withdrawn in December 1934, one month short of 31 years' service. *K. Field / Rail Archive Stephenson*

Above left:
Aston-allocated No 42957 at Birmingham New Street with a train of empty stock in 1957, with a new DMU at Platform 4 (*left*). No 42957 would last until January 1966, putting in just over 32 years of service. *M. Mensing*

Left:
A powerful picture of Crewe South's No 42959 heading away from its home town with an express for Chester and North Wales on 5 September 1957. The locomotive would survive until December 1965. *D. M. C. Hepburne-Scott / Rail Archive Stephenson*

Above:
Looking uncommonly clean,
No 42977 heads an up empty
coal train, south of Harecastle,
on 28 September 1963.
This locomotive was to be one of
the last four of its class in service,
surviving thus until June 1966.
M. Mensing

Right:
Seen south of Bedworth station,
No 42981 of Rugby shed heads a rake
of empty 'Catfish' wagons along the
Coventry–Nuneaton line on 12 May
1964. The locomotive had another
two years of service ahead of it, not
being withdrawn until May 1966.
M. Mensing

Right:

The Stanier Moguls were very rarely used on railtours, but on 29 May 1960 the Stephenson Locomotive Society had No 42952 haul its 'Northern Fells Rail Tour'. Starting from Lancaster Green Ayre, this visited Glasson Dock, thereafter travelling via Clapham Junction, Ingleton, Penrith, Kirkby Stephen and Ulverston to (Windermere) Lakeside. This itinerary involved many miles of tender-first running; in this view at Clapham Junction the locomotive is about to run round prior to heading for Penrith. *Gavin Morrison*

Below:

The tour ran late, but on the section from Kirkby Stephen to Ulverston no less than 28 minutes was regained; this involved some high-speed tender-first running on the West Coast main line between Tebay and Hest Bank, around 75mph being recorded through Oxenholme. Preparing to leave Lakeside at the start of the return journey to Lancaster, No 42952 is seen in company with Fairburn 2-6-4T No 42136, which was also on a weekend special.

Above:
Heading an up cattle train on the North Wales main line on 5 September 1957, No 42971 passes Llandulas, the point at which the four-track section started. The locomotive was to remain in service until December 1964. *K. L. Cook / Rail Archive Stephenson*

Below:
The Stanier 2-6-0s were frequent visitors to Shap. Receiving assistance from the rear, No 42959 passes Scout Green as it attacks the 1-in-75 gradient at the head of a down freight, probably in the early 1950s. The Mogul would survive until December 1965. *W. J. V. Anderson / Rail Archive Stephenson*

On the Eastern and North Eastern Regions

Left:
Leaving Leeds with a local train for Manchester Victoria, No 42964 passes Farnley Junction shed on 17 May 1960. The locomotive would be withdrawn in November 1965.
Gavin Morrison

Below left:
Another local train for Manchester Victoria pulls out of Leeds City, this time headed by No 42970. Unfortunately the photograph is undated, but judging by the carriages it was probably taken in the late 1950s. The locomotive would last until October 1965. *J. W. Hague / N. Stead collection*

Above:
Bound for North Wales with a Summer Saturday extra from Leeds, No 42952 heads away from Batley in the early 1960s, when this was the junction for several lines and there were six platforms; today only the two on the left remain, and there are only two through lines.
K. Field / Rail Archive Stephenson

Left:
Another view of Crewe South's No 42952, here looking well cleaned, as it awaits the signal at the west end of Huddersfield station before entering the tunnel and starting the 1-in-105 climb to Marsden — 7½ miles away — with a freight for Liverpool. The locomotive would remain in service until September 1964. *K. Field / Rail Archive Stephenson*

Right:
As a local train drifts downhill towards Huddersfield the rare combination of a Stanier Mogul — Crewe South's No 42956 — and an unrebuilt 'Patriot' head up the bank towards Marsden with an express bound for Liverpool. No 42956 would be withdrawn in September 1964.
K. Field / Rail Archive Stephenson

Above:
In 1947 there emerged from Horwich Works the first of a radically new type of LMS 2-6-0, designed by the railway's new CME, H. G. Ivatt. The design featured a huge double chimney for a double exhaust, giving the locomotive an austere but powerful appearance, but until modifications were made steaming was far from satisfactory. Only the first three locomotives (Nos 3000-2) received LMS livery, shown in this early view of No 3001. Classification was initially 4F. *Ian Allan Library*

Variations and Liveries

Left:
The next eight locomotives (Nos 3003-10), turned out after Nationalisation, in 1948, received British Railways lettering with 'M' prefix to their numbers. Three were sent to Workington shed, including No M3007, seen here complete with 12D shedplate. *Ian Allan Library*

Right:
After 11 examples had been completed the 'M' number prefix was dropped, all subsequent locomotives being numbered in the new BR scheme, with 40,000 added to their intended LMS numbers. Here the first of the class, No 43000, has just had its number altered. *Ian Allan Library*

Right:
The plain black livery was replaced by the full BR lined version as shown here. Completed in April 1949, No 43031 started its career at Derby. Undated, the photograph must have been taken prior to November 1954, when this locomotive had its double chimney (as fitted originally to Nos 43000-49) replaced by a single one. *Ian Allan Library*

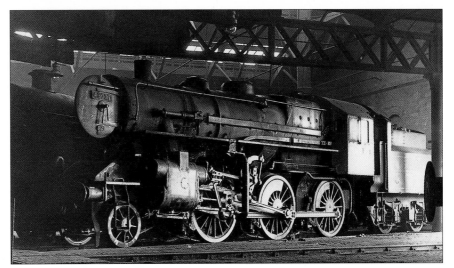

Right:
In 1950, in an attempt to cure the problem of poor steaming, Derby Works fitted No 43027 with a modified single blastpipe and chimney, in which form the locomotive is seen inside Derby shed on 26 April 1953. The modification must have been a success, as between the end of 1953 and 1956 the other 49 locomotives fitted originally with double chimneys would have these replaced, albeit with conventional lipped chimneys as opposed to the rather ugly 'stovepipe' version seen here. *H. C. Casserley*

Right:
A later picture of No 43027, apparently ex works (albeit still with 'BRITISH RAILWAYS' on the tender) and now fitted with conventional single chimney. This locomotive would be one of the last five of the class to be withdrawn, in May 1968. *Ian Allan Library*

Left:
Of the 162 Ivatt Class 4 Moguls, constructed between December 1947 and September 1952, 75 (Nos 43000-49 and 43112-36) were built at Horwich Works, the remainder at Doncaster. Seen at Doncaster shed in 1953, No 43104 displays BR lined-black livery with the first style of lion-and-wheel emblem. Note (on the tender) the tablet-catcher, fitted to locomotives allocated to work on ex-Midland & Great Northern Joint lines. *Gavin Morrison*

Below left:
No 43059 was new to Peterborough New England shed, but by 29 April 1962, when this picture was taken at Doncaster, it was allocated to Boston. Still fitted with a tablet-catcher, it was now in plain unlined black, with the second style of BR lion-and-wheel emblem. *Gavin Morrison*

Bottom left:
Fortunately the lined-black livery returned. No 43112 of Lancaster shed is seen at Leeds Holbeck on 21 June 1961. *Gavin Morrison*

Above right:
Darlington Works used to outshop locomotives with large emblems on their tenders, as demonstrated by recently ex-works No 43129 on shed at Darlington on 11 October 1961. *Gavin Morrison*

Right:
The last of the double-chimney locomotives was No 43049, seen here emerging from Elstree Tunnel with a down goods on 17 May 1952, at which time it was allocated to Derby. It would lose its double chimney in April 1955 and continue in service until August 1967, latterly working from Carlisle Kingmoor.
C. R. L. Coles / Rail Archive Stephenson

Right:
Seen passing Mill Hill on 5 September 1953 at the head of a down slow passenger working, Leicester-allocated No 43018 would retain its double chimney until October 1955 and would remain in service until October 1966, latterly from Stoke shed.
E. R. Wethersett

Below:
Allocated to Staveley Barrow Hill, No 43143 was a long way from home when photographed leaving Northchurch Tunnel (north of Berkhamsted, on the West Ccoast main line) with an up breakdown train on 29 August 1964. The locomotive was on its way to Eastleigh Works for repair but would last only another 10 months before being withdrawn.
Brian Stephenson

Right:

Photographed on 2 July 1948 when only two months old, Nottingham shed's No 43018 prepares to leave Nottingham Victoria station at the head of the 4.35pm to Mansfield. In the background can be seen an ex-LNER Class B17 'Sandringham' 4-6-0. Retaining its double chimney until October 1955, the Mogul would continue in service until October 1966, ending its career at Stoke shed.
T. G. Hepburn / Rail Archive Stephenson

Below:

Another picture at the very photogenic Nottingham Victoria station. One of the class sent new to Melton Constable for working the M&GN lines, No 43152, by now working from Colwick shed, prepares to leave with a local train, probably for Grantham. The locomotive would see out its days at Colwick, being withdrawn in January 1964.
T. G. Hepburn / Rail Archive Stephenson

Above:
Rebuilt with single chimney in December 1954, Saltley-allocated No 43036 receives assistance at the rear from Hawksworth '94xx' 0-6-0PT No 8402 as it climbs the 1-in-37 Lickey Incline at the head of the 9.24am from Great Malvern to Birmingham New Street, formed largely of ex-GWR coaches. Transferred to Workington shed, the Mogul would be withdrawn in May 1966. *M. Mensing*

Below:
Another Saltley-allocated Mogul, No 43040, arrives at Ashchurch on 29 July 1961 with the 5.15pm local train from Bristol Temple Meads to Birmingham New Street. Rebuilt with single chimney in May 1953, it would be withdrawn in November 1966 from North & South Blyth. *M. Mensing*

Right:
Having run round after arriving tender-first with the 5.10pm from Birmingham New Street via Redditch and Evesham, Saltley's No 43017 shunts its now empty stock at Ashchurch on 6 June 1959. The main line to Birmingham and Bristol is in the foreground (right), that to Tewksbury and Great Malvern being on the far right. New to Leeds Holbeck in May 1948, No 43017 lost its double chimney in February 1954 and would eventually be withdrawn from Workington in November 1967. *M. Mensing*

Right:
No 43036 heads a Bristol-bound express near Wincanton in 1949. In 1950 this was one of be three double-chimney Ivatt Class 4 Moguls (the others being Nos 43013 and 43017) transferred to Bath Green Park shed, to work trains on the Somerset & Dorset. However, that line's steep gradients soon found out the type's steaming weaknesses, and by the end of 1950 they had disappeared, never again to work trains south over the Somerset & Dorset — even after all had been rebuilt with single chimneys. Thus modified in December 1954, No 43036 would remain in service until May 1966. *Ian Allan Library*

Right:
The class did put in appearances at Bath Green Park post 1950, but were not used to head trains south from there towards Bournemouth. Saltley-allocated No 43012 leaves the station with a local train — the Saturdays-only 12.20 to Bristol — on 23 June 1962. In the background a Stanier 'Black Five', No 44663, appears ready to come off shed. Rebuilt with single chimney in November 1955, the Mogul would eventually be withdrawn from North & South Blyth in April 1967. *Hugh Ballantyne*

Left:
Depicted on the previous page much earlier in its career, No 43036 (now with single chimney) prepares to leave Birmingham New Street with the 3.5pm to Leicester London Road and Nottingham Midland on 22 September 1962. Note the guardrail on the tender, to prevent crews from getting too close to the wires on electrified lines. *M. Mensing*

Left:
A football excursion from Redditch/King's Norton to the Aston Villa ground at Witton passes Aston station on 30 March 1957. Note the wooden platform. A Saltley locomotive when photographed, No 43017 would end its career at Workington in November 1967. *M. Mensing*

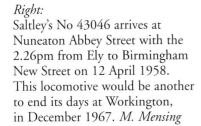

Right:
Saltley's No 43046 arrives at Nuneaton Abbey Street with the 2.26pm from Ely to Birmingham New Street on 12 April 1958. This locomotive would be another to end its days at Workington, in December 1967. *M. Mensing*

Right:
Standing at what was then Platform 8 at Birmingham New Street, having just taken over from BR Standard '4MT' No 75022, Saltley's No 43122 prepares to take a football special from Gloucester forward to Aston Villa's ground at Witton on 16 January 1960. New to Hull Dairycoates in August 1951, this locomotive would end its days at Workington in March 1967. *M. Mensing*

Below:
From the early 1950s a few '43xxx' Moguls were allocated to Cricklewood, one such being No 43019, seen ready to leave St Pancras for Tilbury Riverside with the 3.15pm Swedish Lloyd boat train on 21 October 1961. It got its single chimney in January 1954 and would be one of the last of the class to be withdrawn, from Lostock Hall shed in May 1968. *M. Mensing*

Left:
Night-time photography at Birmingham New Street's Platform 9 and featuring Saltley's No 43017 waiting to depart with the 9.45pm to Worcester Street Hill on 14 March 1957. The fireman looks to be suspended in mid-air as he attends to the steam-heat pipe. *M. Mensing*

Below:
Featured earlier with its unique stovepipe chimney (see page 55), No 43027 had long since been rebuilt with a standard lipped version by the time this photograph was taken. Still allocated to Derby, it is seen arriving at Ambergate station with a local train from Manchester Central to Derby on 10 July 1958. *T. G. Hepburn / Rail Archive Stephenson*

Below:
Passing under the line to Grassington (as well as Ilkley and Arthington), Lancaster's No 43113 leaves Skipton at the head of a Morecambe–Leeds train on 22 August 1959. New to Skipton in March and April 1951, Nos 43112 and 43113 were to remain together throughout their careers, ultimately being withdrawn from Crewe South in September 1967 and August 1966 respectively.
Gavin Morrison

Above:
The Lancaster '4MTs' were seldom clean, and No 43021 was no exception when photographed on 22 August 1959 hauling a nine-coach Leeds City–Morecambe express past Skipton North; on the right of the picture can be seen the locomotive shed. New to Nuneaton in December 1948 and rebuilt with single chimney in April 1954, No 43021 would continue in service until September 1967, ending its career at Crewe South. *Gavin Morrison*

Above:
One of the original trio new to Workington, No 43009 blows off steam as it passes Shap Summit with an up pick-up goods on 24 August 1963. Having lost its double chimney in April 1954, it remained at Workington for the majority of its working career, which was to end at Tebay in November 1966.
Gavin Morrison

Left:
On 25 February 1967 Kingmoor's No 43106 was rostered at Carlisle to take over the 'Border Countryman' railtour, which arrived late behind Holbeck 'Jubilee' No 45562 *Alberta*. In spite of its rather shabby appearance the Mogul regained much of the lost time, thanks largely to fast runs to Beattock and back, during which, it is claimed, it exceeded 80mph. The train is seen crossing the River Eden near Kingmoor. Withdrawn from Lostock Hall in June 1968, No 43106 is the only member of the class preserved and can today be found on the Severn Valley Railway. *Gavin Morrison*

Right:
A large number of '43xxx' Moguls were allocated from new to King's Lynn, Melton Constable and Yarmouth Beach sheds for working services on the former Midland & Great Northern Joint lines, the locomotives in question being fitted with tender-mounted tablet-catchers (as were those new to New England shed at Peterborough). Here a grimy No 43059 arrives at Castle Bytham en route for King's Lynn on August Bank Holiday (5 August) 1957. This locomotive would end its days far from the M&GN, at Staveley Barrow Hill, in January 1965. *M. Mensing*

Below:
On the occasion of his visit to Goole shed on 17 August 1958 the author chanced to have in his pocket some chalk, which he put to good use by highlighting the initials 'M&GN' on the tablet-catcher of Ivatt Class 4 Mogul No 43069, then a Hull Dairycoates engine. *Gavin Morrison*

Above:
Peterborough New England's No 43088 arrives at Tydd with the 9.55am from Murrow East to Hunstanton on Sunday 31 August 1958. Based at New England shed from new (in December 1950) until well into the 1960s, the locomotive would be withdrawn from Lostock Hall in December 1967. *Hugh Ballantyne*

Left:
One of the principal engineering features on the M&GN lines was Sutton swing bridge over the River Nene, which King's Lynn Mogul No 43094 is seen crossing slowly with the 12.58 Peterborough–Yarmouth Beach on 30 August 1958. New to South Lynn shed in December 1950, the locomotive would be transferred to New England following closure of King's Lynn in 1959, being withdrawn from the Peterborough shed in January 1964. The bridge, however, remains in use to this day, having been adapted following the closure of the line to carry road traffic travelling westbound along the A17.
Hugh Ballantyne

Left:
New to Melton Constable in December 1951,
No 43154 shows its 32G shedplate as it passes
through Hillington station with the 9.30am
Peterborough–Yarmouth Beach on 30 August 1958.
Passenger services on the M&GN line were to cease
on 6 April 1964, following which No 43154 would be
transferred away to Colwick shed, near Nottingham,
for its final few months until withdrawal in December
of that year. *Hugh Ballantyne*

Below:
Attached to the front of No 43060, a somewhat
Heath Robinson headboard proclaiming 'That's yer lot'
signifies the last day of through express services over the
M&GN line on 28 February 1959. Seen passing
Little Bytham Junction, the train is the 9.02am
Yarmouth Beach–Birmingham New Street.
No 43060 was a New England locomotive at the time
but would be transferred shortly afterwards to Lincoln
and end its days, in December 1964, at Colwick.
T. G. Hepburn / Rail Archive Stephenson

Right:
On 31 August 1958 the 10.53
Spalding–Hunstanton (Sundays only),
headed by a very dirty Boston-
allocated No 43085, calls at Gedney,
which station was to close on
2 March 1959. New to Peterborough
New England in November 1950,
the locomotive would end its career
in January 1965 at Carnforth shed.
Hugh Ballantyne

On the Eastern and North Eastern Regions

Left:
Taken from the road bridge at the south end of Peterborough station, this picture shows No 43086 standing at Platform 2 with an M&GN train; in the background can be seen the coaling tower for the ex-Midland shed at Spital Bridge, transferred to the Eastern Region in 1950. No 43086 was to spend its entire career based at New England shed, whence it would be withdrawn in December 1964. *N. Stead collection*

Below left:
By 1958 No 43063 was allocated to Woodford Halse, as indicated here by its 38E shedplate. Seen at Leicester Central with an up slow train formed of non-corridor coaches, it would be withdrawn in January 1965 from North Blyth shed. *T. G. Hepburn / Rail Archive Stephenson*

Top right:
No 43145 takes water at Mansfield Town whilst working the RCTS 'Dukeries Tour' from Sheffield Victoria on 24 July 1960. Originally an M&GN locomotive, having been allocated from new (September 1951) to South Lynn, it was by now based at Staveley GC shed but would be withdrawn from Colwick in January 1965. *Gavin Morrison*

Above right:
The morning Newcastle–Liverpool Lime Street, hauled by the most unusual combination of Saltley's No 43036 piloting Holyhead's rebuilt 'Royal Scot' No 46150 *The Life Guardsman*, passes Farnley Junction, Leeds, on the climb to Morley Tunnel on 20 August 1960. No 43036 was one of three double-chimney Moguls which in the early 1950s had worked on the Somerset & Dorset line and had given the crews so much trouble with poor steaming; however, such problems were resolved when it was rebuilt with single chimney, and it would continue in service, latterly from Workington shed, until May 1966. *Gavin Morrison*

Above:
No 43038 is seen in the yard at Calverley & Rodley in charge of a local pick-up goods on 26 February 1958, by which time it must have been the last of its class to retain a double chimney. Having been transferred several times early in its career, the locomotive was now allocated to Stourton shed, where it would remain until withdrawn in May 1964. *Gavin Morrison*

Above:
No 43044 passes Wortley Junction, Leeds, with an up train of empty coal wagons on 26 September 1963, by which time the '4MTs' were taking over from the Midland '4F' 0-6-0s that had worked these trains since before the war. Having spent many years at Stourton shed, this locomotive would end its career at Leeds Holbeck, in September 1967. *Gavin Morrison*

Below:
Another picture of Stourton's No 43038, now fitted with a single chimney, passing Whitehall Junction, Leeds, with a down local freight on 6 February 1964, three months before withdrawal. *Gavin Morrison*

Right:
One of Manningham shed's Fairburn 2-6-4Ts, No 42072, pilots Lancaster's No 43021 at the head of a Leeds–Morecambe express on the morning of 15 August 1959. Apparently made up of non-corridor coaches, the train, having just passed Guiseley Junction, is approaching the sharp curve at Shipley. New to Nuneaton shed in December 1948, No 43021 later moved on to Devons Road, Bow, and in April 1954 was rebuilt with single chimney, in which form it would remain in service, latterly from Crewe South, until September 1967. *Gavin Morrison*

Left:
Allocated to Ardsley at the time, No 43072 ended its career in spectacular fashion in November 1964 when it ran away down the steep gradient into Bradford Adolphus Street goods yard with an unfitted freight. Fortunately the crew had the sense to jump off before the locomotive went through the wall and plunged about 20ft or more into the street below, nearly hitting a passing car. A scrap merchant was called in to cut the locomotive on site, which work is shown in progress on 11 November. *Gavin Morrison*

Right:
Allocated to South Lynn when new in July 1951, No 43137 was soon transferred to Eastfield shed in Glasgow, where it remained until the early 1960s. From *c*1964 it had a spell at Copley Hill, from which shed it was working when photographed on 2 July 1966 with the Bradford Exchange portion of an express from King's Cross, which had just come off the Leeds-avoiding side of the triangle at Wortley West Junction. The locomotive would end its days at North & South Blyth shed in September 1967. *Gavin Morrison*

Left:
Manningham's No 43030 takes the Bradford line around the Shipley triangle at Bingley Junction on 20 April 1961 with a local pick-up goods bound for Valley Road goods yard. Still allocated to Manningham, it would eventually be withdrawn in October 1966. *Gavin Morrison*

Left:
Its mis-shapen cab suggesting some kind of mishap, No 43140 keeps company with Kingmoor 'Britannia' No 70036 *Boadicea* on shed at Manningham on 23 June 1966. New to Polmont, on the Scottish Region, in August 1951 and moving to St Rollox in the early 1960s, the '4MT' had had a spell at Darlington in 1964 before being transferred to Normanton, where its career was to end in May 1967. *Gavin Morrison*

Left:
Holbeck-allocated No 43130 arrives tender-first at Leeds Central from Copley Hill carriage sidings with the empty stock for the 11.30am to King's Cross on 3 January 1967. Leeds Central would close just four months later, on 1 May, the '4MT' surviving until June. *M. Dunnett*

Right:
Another view of No 43137 on the Bradford portion of an express from King's Cross, this time on 8 July 1966. The train is descending the 1-in-50 gradient through the deep cutting at St Dunstans, on the outskirts of Bradford. The lines branching off in the foreground formed a triangle and eventually led onto the old Great Northern route to Queensbury, Keighley and Halifax. *Gavin Morrison*

Right:
Coming off the Scarborough line with a local pick-up goods, Hull Dairycoates' No 43053 enters York station in the early 1950s. Bisecting the East Coast main line at right angles, Waterworks Crossing, over which the train is passing, has long since been removed. The locomotive was to remain based on the North Eastern Region throughout its career, which would end at Manningham in April 1964. *Ian Allan Library*

Above:
Heading a local train from Leeds City to York in the early 1950s, Selby's No 43052 passes the site of Marsh Lane station (closed to passengers from 15 September 1958) prior to entering the deep cutting out to Neville Hill. The locomotive's career was to end at Crewe South shed in November 1966. *K. Field / Rail Archive Stephenson*

Left:
New England's No 43065 is a long way from home as it passes the signalbox at Northallerton *c*1955 with an up fitted freight — more typically the responsibility of an ex-LNER Class V2 2-6-2. Note (on the locomotive's tender) the tablet-catcher for working the M&GN lines. One of a batch of 12 delivered to New England in late 1950 (in this case September), No 43065 would be withdrawn from Colwick in January 1965. *J. W. Hague / N. Stead collection*

Left:
Allocated to Hull Dairycoates (to which shed it had been new in February 1951) No 43100 sets off for Scarborough after collecting a few wagons at Seamer on 21 July 1958. It remained on the North Eastern Region throughout its career, which would come to an end at West Hartlepool in February 1967. *M. Mensing*

Right:
Another view of Selby's No 43052, here entering Beverley — note the Minster looming in the background — with the 10.40am Hull–Scarborough on 17 August 1950, at which time the locomotive was less than a month old. *P. Connonley*

Right:
The NER-allocated members of the class were no strangers to the scenic Middlesbrough–Whitby–Scarborough line. No 43071, of Darlington shed, heads the 9.42 West Hartlepool–Scarborough along the coast between Sandsend and Whitby West Cliff on 16 July 1957. The locomotive would continue in service until March 1967, ultimately being withdrawn from North & South Blyth. *M. Mensing*

Below:
An unidentified Ivatt '4MT' crosses the impressive Larpool Viaduct (near Whitby) with the 9.44 Middlesbrough–Scarborough on 19 July 1957. Passenger services on the Scarborough–Whitby line would finish on 5 March 1965. *M. Mensing*

Right:
Seen in the mid-1950s when based at Middlesbrough, No 43051 approaches Prospect Hill 'box, Whitby, with a Scarborough–Middlesbrough train. In the background is Larpool Viaduct over the River Esk, while on the right is a train of empty stock descending the spur to Whitby Town station. Note that, unusually, the North Eastern signals are not mounted on slatted posts. No 43051 would continue in service until January 1967, ending its career at Manningham shed. *A. M. Ross*

Left:
The Ivatt '4MT' 2-6-0s were well used on the famous Stainmore line across the Pennines, on both passenger and freight workings. Here No 43018 receives banking assistance as it climbs towards Stainmore Summit (1,370ft) with a coke train for Cumbria. Allocated to Workington when this photograph was taken, it had lost its double chimney in October 1955 and after various transfers would end its career at Stoke, in October 1966. *C. Ord collection*

Left:
With guardrail on the tender, No 43049 passes Kirkby Stephen East station, with all but one line removed, with the local freight from Carlisle to Merrygill Quarry on 16 July 1965, the final passenger train having departed on 22 January 1962. Rebuilt with single chimney in April 1955, No 43049 would end its career at Carlisle Kingmoor, in August 1967. *D. Cross*

Right:
Piloting BR Standard '3MT' 2-6-2T No 82028, Ivatt '4MT' No 43101 arrives at Tebay with the 7.23am South Shields–Blackpool on 30 June 1956. A North Eastern Region locomotive for its entire career, the Mogul would be withdrawn from North & South Blyth in March 1967. *J. E. Wilkinson*

Above:
Running tender-first at the head of a coal train from the Durham collieries, No 43057 encounters English Electric Type 4 diesel No D349, in charge of the 12.00 Newcastle–Colchester, on 26 August 1966. Both trains are approaching Hart station, just north of Hartlepool, this being the point at which the line from Wingate (*left*) joined the coast line from Sunderland (*right*). Allocated to West Hartlepool at the time of the photograph, No 43057 would remain based at that shed until withdrawn in December 1966. *J. H. Bird*

Left:
With a fine reflection visible in the carriage windows, No 43015 descends from Fawcett Street Junction to Sunderland at the head of a train from Blackpool to South Shields (via Stainmore) on 15 August 1959. The locomotive was then allocated to West Hartlepool, at which shed it would end its career in July 1967. *I. S. Carr*

Below left:
Passing through the kind of industrial landscape once so typical of the area, No 43100, a West Hartlepool engine, approaches Stockton-on-Tees station with a mixed freight on 27 September 1966. It would be withdrawn the following February. *M. Mensing*

Above right:
In a superb setting, No 43121 crosses Lambley Viaduct, on the Haltwhistle–Alston branch, with the SLS 'Scottish Rambler' railtour on Easter Sunday (26 March) 1967. The locomotive would continue in service at Carlisle Kingmoor until November. Part of the Alston branch, which would close to passengers with effect from 3 May 1976, has now been reopened as the 2ft-gauge South Tynedale Railway. *A. G. Cattle*

Right:
A fine picture of the 6.12pm Sunderland–West Hartlepool stopping train, headed by No 43128, leaving Ryhope East on 3 May 1958. The '4MT' was by then allocated to West Hartlepool, where it would remain in service until July 1965. *I. S. Carr*

Right:
Passing an English Electric Type 3 diesel in the sidings, No 43123 approaches Hartburn Junction, Stockton-on-Tees, with an up freight on 15 May 1965. Although impossible to decipher from the shedplate, the Mogul's allocation is likely to have been West Hartlepool, although the locomotive would be transferred to North & South Blyth ahead of withdrawal in July 1967. *T. G. Hepburn / Rail Archive Stephenson*

On the Scottish Region

Above:
New to Carlisle Canal in July 1951, No 43139 spent its entire career allocated to the Border City, transferring to Kingmoor upon closure of Canal in 1963. Nearly always rostered to trains on the Langholm branch, it is seen at the terminus on 30 June 1956. The branch was to close from 15 June 1964, but No 43139 would continue in service until September 1967.
Hugh Ballantyne

Left:
On 10 October 1963 No 43139 must have been receiving a washout or under repair, for on that day its regular turns were being covered by older classmate No 43011, seen ready to leave Langolm with the 3.28pm for Carlisle. New to Derby in March 1948 with double chimney, this locomotive had been rebuilt in June 1953 and would be withdrawn from Workington in February 1967.
Hugh Ballantyne

Right:
Already featured opposite, No 43139 seldom ventured far from Carlisle, but in May 1962 it was photographed pssing Arkleston Junction, Paisley, in charge of a pick-up goods. *D. Cross*

Below:
No 43133 heads a train of non-corridor coaches away from Joppa, to the east of Edinburgh, on the suburban circle line, on 16 July 1960. By this date the locomotive was allocated to Kipps, but it would be withdrawn from North & South Blyth, in December 1966.
G. M. Staddon / N. Stead collection

Right:
New to Glasgow Eastfield in December 1951, No 43135 stayed for more than 10 years, working suburban services along the north side of the River Clyde, in addition to general freight. Here it is leaving Craigendoran Lower on 11 August 1960 with a train for Glasgow Queen Street; on the right can be seen Craigendoran Upper, on the West Highland line. Eventually transferred to Manningham shed, Bradford, the '4MT' would be withdrawn in October 1966.
Gavin Morrison

Variations and Liveries

Left:
At the end of World War 2 the LMS was faced with an urgent need for a branch-line locomotive to replace several hundred ageing 0-6-0s. New CME H. G. Ivatt persuaded the authorities that a 2-6-0 wheel arrangement would be far superior to an 0-6-0 in terms of ride quality, and so it proved, the Class 2 Moguls being well liked throughout the Locomotive Department for their ease of servicing as well as performance. The first 20 locomotives, Nos 6400-19, were built at Crewe Works by the LMS between December 1946 and March 1947, the rest after nationalisation. Livery was plain black with straw-coloured numerals and lettering, of sanserif type. No 6417 is seen at an unidentified shed, possibly Bank Hall, Liverpool, its first allocation. *Ian Allan Library*

Below:
Like the larger Class 4s, the Class 2 Moguls initially proved less than satisfactory in service. In 1951, in an effort to improve draughting, No 46413 was sent to Swindon Works, while No 46424 received this 'stovepipe' chimney during tests at Derby, which resulted in the fitting of a slender chimney to locomotives under construction at Darlington in 1951/2. *H. C. Casserley*

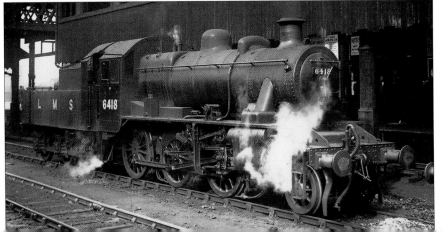

Below left:
Nos 6418 and 6419 were the last of the Ivatt 2-6-0s to enter service under LMS ownership, in March 1947. Both were allocated to Newton Heath shed, Manchester, and could be seen for many years at Manchester Victoria awaiting a banking duty up Miles Platting Bank. The first 20 (Nos 6400-19) entered service in plain black, with straw and maroon lettering and numbers. No 6418 would survive until November 1967, still allocated to Newton Heath. *W. H. Whitworth / Rail Archive Stephenson*

Right:
No 46484, one of the Darlington-built locomotives, in lined black with early BR emblem. The tall, narrow chimney was fitted to Nos 46465-89. *Ian Allan Library*

Left:
The second of its class to be built by BR, at Crewe in November 1948, No 46421 was turned out in plain black, with 'BRITISH RAILWAYS' on the tender. *Ian Allan Library*

Right:
In due course the plain black was replaced by lined black, as seen in this later picture of No 46434. *Ian Allan Library*

Left:
No 46460 emerged from Crewe in May 1950 in lined black with the early lion-and-wheel emblem. *Ian Allan Library*

Right:
A fine study of No 46402, by now with the second lion-and-wheel emblem, outside its home shed at Derby on 14 October 1962.
Brian Stephenson

Below:
A comparison between the Darlington narrow chimney (*right*) and that eventually fitted to the rest of the class by Crewe and Swindon works.
Nos 46431 and 46486 are seen on 9 October 1965 at their then home depot of Lancaster. *Gavin Morrison*

Right:
The final batch of 25 locomotives was built at Swindon Works in 1952/3. Some 22 of this batch (Nos 46503-24) were allocated initially to Oswestry, from where they handled most of the secondary traffic on the Cambrian lines for around 10 years, but the final three (Nos 46525-7) were new to Bristol St Philip's Marsh. Later transferred to Watford, where this photograph was taken in 1963, No 46526 is pictured still in the lined-green livery applied latterly to WR-allocated locomotives. *P. Russell / Rail Archive Stephenson*

Right:
From the late 1950s some overhauled locomotives returned to traffic in plain black. One such was No 46498, which, judging by the large crest and numerals, must have been treated at Darlington. It is seen at Holbeck shed, Leeds, on 12 April 1962. *Gavin Morrison*

Right:
The class was allocated to all regions of BR except the Southern. A clean No 46466, then based at Cambridge, passes Cambridge South signalbox as it departs with the 9.35am excursion train to Colchester via the Colne Valley line on 22 June 1958. Note that by this date the locomotive had lost its original narrow chimney. Only ever allocated to Cambridge and March, it would end its career at the latter, in August 1962. *K. L. Cook / Rail Archive Stephenson*

Right:
By contrast with No 46466 in the previous picture No 46467 still had its Darlington narrow chimney on 24 May 1959, when it was photographed leaving its home city of Cambridge with an excursion to Clacton. Having spent most of its time at Cambridge, this locomotive would eventually be transferred to Dumfries, where it was to end its days in July 1964. *D. M. C. Hepburne-Scott / Rail Archive Stephenson*

On the London Midland Region

Above:
Approaching Stechford station, on the line to Aston, No 46446 is seen heading a rake of non-corridor stock provided for the football special from Coventry to Witton, on the occasion of the Aston Villa v Sheffield Wednesday match on 13 April 1958. A Coventry locomotive at the time, the '2MT' was to end up at Shrewsbury, from where it would be withdrawn in December 1966. *M. Mensing*

Right:
On the last day of service between Redditch and Evesham, 29 September 1962, No 46492 leaves Redditch with the 1.12pm from Birmingham New Street. Allocated to Aston for most of its career, it would end its days at Buxton, in June 1967. *M. Mensing*

Right:
Still with Darlington narrow chimney, No 46470 climbs Hatton Bank with a down oil train on 12 March 1966. Latterly allocated to Workington, it would be withdrawn in May 1967. *M. Mensing*

Right:
Looking as if it has been prepared for some special turn, possibly a Royal Train, No 46427 engages in mundane duties as it shunts the siding at Stechford station on 17 March 1962. At the time allocated to Aston, it was to spend its entire career based in the Birmingham area, ultimately being withdrawn from Tyseley in October 1966. *M. Mensing*

Left:
Rebuilding is in progress at the west end of Birmingham New Street as No 46448 of Saltley shed arrives with a short parcels train on 30 July 1964. Later transferred to Newton Heath, Manchester, the locomotive would be withdrawn in May 1967. *M. Mensing*

Above:
Ready to depart with an SLS special, Swindon-built
No 46522 stands at Birmingham New Street's Platform 3
on 2 November 1963; on the left is a Metro-Cammell
DMU (later Class 101) forming the 2.52pm to Four Oaks.
Having spent most of its working career allocated to either
Oswestry or Brecon, the '2MT' would end up at Carnforth,
surviving there until May 1967. *M. Mensing*

Below:
Another non-corridor football special approaches Stechford
en route from Coventry to Witton, this time for the
Aston Villa *v* Nottingham Forest game on 6 September
1958. The locomotive is again Coventry's No 46446.
M. Mensing

Above:
One of the LMS-built members of the class, No 46404 arrives at Long Stanton on 20 July 1957. Then allocated to Kettering, the locomotive would end its days at Aintree in May 1965. The station, on the Kettering–Cambridge line, would close to passengers on 5 October 1970. *A. R. Carpenter / N. Stead collection*

Right:
In LMS livery and with original '2F' power classification on the cabside, the third of the class to be built, No 6402, stands proudly at Nottingham Victoria on 15 May 1948, its 15B shedplate denoting allocation to Kettering. It is fitted with a Stanier-type chimney, which would later be replaced by the slightly taller standard type. Renumbered 46402 by BR, this locomotive would remain in service until July 1967, latterly from Buxton shed. *T. G. Hepburn / Rail Archive Stephenson*

Right:
Another of the LMS-built locomotives, No 6416 leaves the north end of Nottingham Victoria on 1 July 1948 with the 4.35pm for Mansfield. Like No 6402 in the previous picture it appears very clean after more than a year in service and retains its '2F' cabside classification and Stanier-type chimney. It would survive until April 1966, its final allocation being Bolton. *T. G. Hepburn / Rail Archive Stephenson*

Above:
In a terrible state externally, No 46494 calls at Dore & Totley station with the 12.35 from Sheffield Midland to Chinley via the Hope Valley on 3 October 1959, at which time it was allocated to Sheffield Millhouses. This locomotive would be one of the earliest members of the class to be withdrawn, from March shed in September 1962. *M. Mensing*

Left:
No 46440 approaches Chee Tor No 2 Tunnel, west of Millers Dale, on Easter Monday (2 April) 1956 with the 1.5pm Derby–Buxton local. Having spent most of its career working (as here) from Derby shed, it would end its days at Newton Heath, in March 1967. *M. Mensing*

Above:

The Ivatt '2MTs' were a familiar sight at Manchester Victoria from March 1947, when Nos 6418 and 6419 were allocated new to Newton Heath, until virtually the end of BR steam. They were usually used as the Miles Platting bankers, No 46411 being shown awaiting its next such duty on 27 March 1956. This particular locomotive was to spend at least 12 years based at Newton Heath, culminating in its withdrawal in January 1967. *N. Stead collection*

Right:

An immaculate No 46496, one of the Darlington-built locomotives, passes Chesterton Junction with a train from Kettering to Cambridge on 28 April 1959. Having spent more than eight years allocated to Kettering, it would be withdrawn in March 1966 from Liverpool Bank Hall.
D. M. C. Hepburne-Scott / Rail Archive Stephenson

Above:
New to Skipton shed in February 1950, No 46440 is pictured leaving Earby station, on the now closed Skipton–Colne line, with a Skipton–Preston passenger train on 30 July 1952. The locomotive is fitted with one of the Stanier-type chimneys, which would be replaced by a slightly slimmer but taller version seen on No 46452 in the following picture.
C. R. L. Coles / Rail Archive Stephenson

Left:
Another Skipton engine, No 46452 passes Skipton North signalbox as it leaves its home town and heads towards Earby with a train for Blackburn on 22 August 1959. The '2MTs' could certainly run fast when required, and it was when travelling behind this locomotive, on a two-coach train between Keighley and Skipton, that the author recorded an average speed of almost 60mph from start to stop, passing Connonley station at 73mph! Remaining in the Bradford/Skipton area until at least 1960, No 46452 was to end its days at Workington shed, in May 1967. *Gavin Morrison*

Right:
On 3 December 1966, the last day of service on the Ramsbottom–Bacup line, a special organised by the Locomotive Club of Great Britain ran from West Yorkshire to Bacup, where this picture was taken. Motive power was provided by Newton Heath shed, Ivatt 2-6-0 No 46437 double-heading Stanier 2-6-2T No 42644. The train is seen at Bacup, waiting for the regular DMU-operated service (right) to depart before commencing its return journey. No 46437 would see out its days at Newton Heath, being withdrawn in May 1967.
Gavin Morrison

Above:
New to Preston in December 1948 in BR lined black with 'BRITISH RAILWAYS' on the tender, No 46430 was still based at its original shed in July 1952, when it was photographed shunting carriages at Preston station. In the background is one of Crewe North's double-chimney Class 5MT ('Black Five') 4-6-0s. Subsequently transferred to Stoke shed, the Mogul would end its career at Nuneaton, in October 1965. *D. T. Greenwood / Rail Archive Stephenson*

Left:
Of the 25 Class 2 2-6-0s
(Nos 46503-27) built at Swindon
between November 1952 and March
1953, some 22 were allocated from
new to Oswestry shed, being used on
the Cambrian lines to replace ageing
'Dean Goods' 0-6-0s, the more
modern 'Dukedog' 4-4-0s and various
other ex-Great Western types that
worked in this division; they also
worked trains on the ex-Midland line
between Three Cocks Junction and
Hereford, replacing ex-Lancashire
& Yorkshire 0-6-0s, and were much
appreciated by all departments.
On 10 September 1962 No 46521,
in lined green, arrives at Talyllyn
Junction on the Mid-Wales line and
heads for Brecon on ex-Brecon &
Merthyr metals. This locomotive was
to remain on the Cambrian lines
until withdrawn from Machynlleth
in October 1966 and is now preserved
on the Great Central Railway.
Gavin Morrison

On Cambrian Lines

Above:
Trains passing at Hay-on-Wye on 10 June 1960. Ivatt '2MT' 2-6-0 No 46506 is in charge of the 4.5 from Hereford to
Brecon, whilst heading in the opposite direction is the 4.10 from Brecon to Hereford, hauled by ex-Great Western '57xx'
0-6-0PT No 3662. Services on this line would be withdrawn on 31 December 1962, No 46506 leaving Oswestry
at around the same time and eventually being withdrawn from Newton Heath in May 1967. *Hugh Ballantyne*

Right:

The scene at Brecon station on 28 December 1962. Ivatt '2MT' 2-6-0 No 46512 has just arrived with the 9.2 from Hereford, while on the left ex-Great Western 0-6-0PT No 9616 is leaving with the 12.10pm for Newport. This was at the start of the great winter of 1962/3, and within the next few days all the lines around Brecon would be closed due to the weather. Transferred away from Oswestry *c*1964, No 46512 would end its BR career at Crewe South shed in November 1966 but survives in preservation on the Speyside Railway in Scotland. *Hugh Ballantyne*

Right:

Llanidloes, the main station on the Mid-Wales line, had an impressive station building, goods shed and engine shed, the last (on the right of this picture) being a sub-shed to Oswestry. Seen arriving on 7 June 1960 with the 5.40pm from Moat Lane Junction to Builth Wells, '2MT' No 46523 spent its days on the Cambrian lines allocated to Oswestry or Brecon but would be withdrawn in May 1967 from Aintree. The trackbed at Llanidloes now forms the basis for the town's by-pass, although the station building survives. *Hugh Ballantyne*

Right:

Another view of No 46506, this time at Eardisley on 6 June 1960 with the 10.25 Brecon–Hereford; local signalman Watkins has a chat with the crew before departure. The wooden building (on the left) would survive the station's closure on 31 December 1962, eventually being transported to Welshpool, and is today the main station building at Raven Square. *Hugh Ballantyne*

Left:
Three Cocks Junction was where the Mid-Wales line from Moat Lane joined the ex-Midland line from Hereford and then continued to Talyllyn Junction. It was a fine country station complete with refreshment room, as seen in this picture of No 46511, which has just arrived from Hereford on 11 September 1962. Services would cease at the end of that year, but No 46511 would stay at Oswestry until at least 1964, eventually moving to Shrewsbury until withdrawal in September 1965, having spent its entire life of just under 13 years working on the Cambrian lines. *Gavin Morrison*

Above:
A London Midland Region locomotive from new, No 46446 had only a short spell on the Cambrian lines, being transferred to Machynlleth shed in 1963 when the LMR assumed responsibility for the ex-Cambrian network. Seen arriving at Caersus on 19 August 1963 with the 4.25pm Newton–Machynlleth stopping train, it would continue in service, latterly from Shrewsbury, until December 1966. *M. J. Fox / Rail Archive Stephenson*

Above:
No 46503 arrives at Builth Road Low Level, on the Mid-Wales line, on 2 July 1959 with the 2.5pm Moat Lane–Brecon as a freight train passes through the High Level station on the Central Wales line. The impressive station nameboard informs passengers of the destinations for which they need to change. Turned out in November 1952 as the first of the Swindon build, No 46503 was still an Oswestry locomotive when photographed but would ultimately be withdrawn from Newton Heath, in May 1967. Services on the Mid-Wales line would cease on 31 December 1962, but the High Level station (now simply 'Builth Road') remains open. *R. O. Tuck / Rail Archive Stephenson*

Below:
No 46509 heads along the Cambrian coast near Towyn on 18 March 1963 with a train from Machynlleth to Barmouth; why this should include two sleeping cars (at the rear) is a mystery. No 46509 would shortly leave the Cambrian lines for Tyseley, its final shed before withdrawal in October 1966. *D. M. C. Hepburne-Scott / Rail Archive Stephenson*

Above:
On the frosty morning of
19 December 1964 No 46446
enters Drws-y-Nant, on the line
from Barmouth Junction to Ruabon.
Services on the line would finish
one month later, on 18 January 1965.
Gavin Morrison

Left:
Ivatt '2MT' No 46521 assists
BR Standard '4MT' No 75053
up the final 1-in-52 ascent to
Talerddig Summit with the 6.5pm
Aberystwyth–Shrewsbury on 7 May
1966. Having spent its entire career
working the Cambrian lines,
the Mogul was by now just five
months from withdrawal but
would nevertheless outlast
No 75053. *M. Mensing*

On the Eastern and North Eastern Regions

Above:
The first batch of '2MT' Moguls constructed at Darlington (Nos 46465-82) were all allocated from new to the North Eastern Region. West Auckland's No 46473, with Darlington narrow chimney, coasts through Rose Carr, Darlington, with a freight from Shildon on 26 April 1955. This locomotive would be withdrawn in December 1963, its final allocation being Goole. *R. K. Evans*

Right:
LMS-built No 46415, by now a Wakefield engine, has an easy task heading a Knottingley–Wakefield pick-up goods past Pontefract Tanshelf on 2 May 1958. The locomotive was to remain based in the area for the rest of its career, being withdrawn from Goole in October 1962. *P. Cookson / N. Stead collection*

Right:
Sheffield Millhouses-allocated No 46494 approaches York Holgate *c*1959. Although the lamps suggest an express, the nine-coach train is in fact a stopping service from Sheffield. One of the later Darlington-built locomotives, with standard chimney, No 46494 would be withdrawn (from March shed) in September 1962, after a career of less than 11 years. *P. Cookson / N. Stead collection*

Left:
No 46475, with narrow Darlington chimney, prepares to leave Tebay for Kirkby Stephen in the days when the North Eastern side of the station had an overall roof; unfortunately a precise date is not available, but the photograph appears to date from the early 1950s. Having been allocated to Darlington for nearly all of its career, No 46475 would bow out at Dumfries, in July 1964.
N. Stead collection

Left:
Headed by Kirkby Stephen's No 46471, the Fridays-only 8.42am Ulverston–Durham miners' special (train W515) gets away from Tebay after a locomotive change on 6 June 1952. Tebay station is away to the left of the picture. By the time of its withdrawal in October 1962 No 46471 would be allocated to Tweedmouth. *E. D. Bruton / Rail Archive Stephenson*

Left:
Situated just to the west of Penrith on the ex-Cockermouth, Keswick & Penrith line is Blencow. The goods facilities at the station closed on 1 June 1964, but private sidings remained in use to service Flusco Lime Works, where No 46426 is seen shunting. Allocated to Carlisle Upperby, the locomotive would be withdrawn in September 1966. *N. Stead collection*

Above:
Bound for West Auckland with a mixed goods on 28 May 1960, Ivatt '2MT' No 46422 is banked up to Stainmore Summit by '4MT' No 43018, the train being pictured crossing the famous Belah Viaduct. Designed by Thomas Bouch and built in 1859, the structure was 1,040ft long, 196ft high and cost £31,630; it would be demolished in 1963, 18 months after closure of the line. A Widnes locomotive for most of its career, No 46422 would be withdrawn from Carnforth in December 1966, having survived No 43018 by a couple of months. *J. Spencer Gilkes*

Right:
In a delightful sylvan setting about two miles east of Keswick an unidentified '2MT' 2-6-0 runs tender-first back to Penrith with a special from the Keswick Games one fine evening in August 1965.
W. J. V. Anderson / Rail Archive Stephenson

Left:
On 4 September 1960 the West Riding branch of the RCTS ran its 'Cumbrian Railtour' from Leeds to Penrith via the Cumbrian coast. Haulage was provided successively by the preserved Midland Compound, unrebuilt 'Patriot' No 45503 and two Ivatt '2MTs' — Nos 46442 and 46456 — immaculately turned out by Workington for the trip thence to Penrith; the itinerary also included a trip on the miniature Ravenglass & Eskdale Railway. This view from the footplate of No 46456 shows a DMU passing at Penrudduck. The locomotives put up a very lively performance on the ex-CK&P line, regaining 30 minutes of lost time. At Penrith the Compound would take over for the return leg to Leeds via the Settle–Carlisle line, reaching 87mph at Settle on the descent from Blea Moor. *Gavin Morrison*

Left and below left:
On 13 June 1964 another West Riding RCTS special ran from Penrith to Workington, having arrived from Leeds behind Southern 'Merchant Navy' Pacific No 35012 *United States Lines*. Nos 46426 and 46458 took the train to Workington, where passengers transferred to a DMU to 'do' local lines, the '2MTs' returning to Carlisle via Penrith with those preferring to stay with steam. These two pictures show them on the return journey, firstly just east of Keswick, starting the climb towards Troutbeck, and later near the top of the climb, working hard as they pass Troutbeck with the nine-coach load. Both locomotives would be withdrawn from Carlisle Upperby, in September and December 1966 respectively. *Gavin Morrison*

Right:
A remarkable line-up at Oban on 12 May 1962. On the left of the picture is a special for Glasgow headed by the preserved Caledonian Single and North British 4-4-0 *Glen Douglas*. At the adjacent platform is a BRCW/Sulzer Type 2 (later Class 27) diesel on a more mundane Glasgow train, while shunting stock on the right is '2MT' No 46468, recently transferred from Cambridge to Oban to work the Balluchulish branch. The Mogul would be withdrawn from Grangemouth in October 1965. *Gavin Morrison*

On the Scottish Region

Below right:
Following a short spell at St Margarets Nos 46460 and 46461 were allocated to Kittybrewster shed at Aberdeen, but one was usually to be found at Fraserburgh sub-shed, responsible for working the St Coombes branch. Fitted with cowcatcher guard, No 46460 is seen in the yard at Fraserburgh on 20 May 1952. Later replaced on such work by a BR Standard Class 2MT ('78xxx') 2-6-0, No 46460 would end its days at Ayr, in August 1966. *N. W. Sprinks / N. Stead collection*

Below:
A long-distance transfer involved No 46467, reallocated in the early 1960s from Cambridge (see page 87) to Dumfries and seen at Whauphill, between Newton Stewart and Whithorn, on 26 April 1963. Passenger services on the Whithorn branch had ended on 25 September 1950, but freight would continue until 5 October 1964. *D. Cross*

Left:
This fine study shows Nuneaton-based 'Crab' No 42817 awaiting its turn at the Willesden coaler on 14 May 1955. The locomotive would serve until April 1965.
C. R. L. Coles / Rail Archive Stephenson

Right:
Having just returned 'home' from overhaul at Horwich Works, No 42789 awaits its next duty from Farnley Junction shed on 1 June 1962. It would later be transferred to the Scottish Region, working coal trains around Ayr until withdrawn in November 1966. *Gavin Morrison*

Above:
Carlisle Kingmoor's 'Crabs' were frequent visitors to Leeds Holbeck. No 42882, with large number (as applied by St Rollox Works) and small crest was photographed on 21 August 1961. The locomotive would be withdrawn in December 1962. *Gavin Morrison*

Above:
In 1963 pioneering LMS 2-6-0
No 42700 was allocated to Bury,
being shown here awaiting servicing
at Llandudno Junction shed after
working a special from Lancashire on
22 June. Withdrawn in March 1966,
this locomotive is nowadays part of
the National Collection.
Gavin Morrison

Left:
Dumfries-allocated 'Crab' No 42919
stands outside Stranraer shed on
Sunday 2 July 1961, on which date
there were no locomotives in steam.
Transferred to Dumfries in 1950, it
would be withdrawn in October 1966.
Gavin Morrison

Left:
Although rarely to be seen at Leeds
Holbeck shed, the Stanier 2-6-0s were
frequent visitors to Farnley Junction;
on 30 April 1962 Crewe South's
No 42948 keeps company with native
'WD' 2-8-0 No 90588. The Mogul
would continue in service until
October 1965. *Gavin Morrison*

Above:
Ivatt Class 4 No 43039 over the
ashpits at Holbeck shed, where it was
destined to remain allocated for its
entire career, from July 1949 until
December 1966. This scene was
recorded on 9 July 1960.
Gavin Morrison

Right:
One of the early Ivatt Class 4
locomotives, with double chimney,
No 43020 stands outside its home
shed of Devons Road, Bow, in 1953.
Rebuilt with single chimney in July
1954, it would continue in service
until October 1966, latterly from
Crewe South. Devons Road shed
would be the first in the country to
go all-diesel, in 1958. *Gavin Morrison*

Left:
No 43044 was a Stourton engine for most of its career but was transferred to Holbeck when the former closed. Seen (with painted 55B shedcode) on shed at Manningham on 21 March 1967, it would last only another six months, until September. *Gavin Morrison*

Left:
New to St Margarets shed, Edinburgh, in June 1950, Ivatt '2MT' No 46461 is seen on 14 August 1951 on shed at nearby Haymarket alongside one of the Scottish 'Director' 4-4-0s, No 62678 *Lucy Mucklebackit.* Later transferred to the one-time Great North of Scotland shed at Kittybrewster, No 46461 would ultimately return south to Bathgate, whence it would be withdrawn in July 1964. *D. T. Greenwood / Rail Archive Stephenson*

Left:
The last of the Darlington-built '2MTs' to be fitted with the narrow 'coffee-pot' chimney, No 46489 is seen on 19 June 1960 on shed at Carlisle Upperby, from where it would be withdrawn in November 1963. *Gavin Morrison*

LMS in Preservation

Right:
For several years from around 1968 the National Railway Museum's 'Crab', No 42700, was loaned to the Keighley & Worth Valley Railway, being seen bursting out of Mytholmes Tunnel with a train from Keighley to Oxenhope on 27 October 1968. Having encountered considerable difficulties (caused by malfunctioning sanders) on 'Santa' specials later that year it would see little subsequent work but would remain on the KWVR until returned to the NRM by BR Standard '9F' 2-10-0 No 92220 *Evening Star* on 20 May 1977. It has not been steamed since.
Gavin Morrison

Right:
Stanier Class 5 2-6-0 No 2968 has travelled extensively on the rail network since moving under its own steam for the first time in preservation on 12 November 1990 and has been unofficially christened the 'Mighty Mogul' in recognition of its exceptional railtour performances, which have far exceeded those achieved by the type in regular BR service. For most of its time in preservation it has run with a full-width Stanier tender, altering its appearance considerably. The locomotive is seen thus on 21 December 1996, passing Farington Junction *en route* for Blackburn and the Settle & Carlisle with the 'Christmas Cumbrian Mountain Express'. Note the LNWR-liveried Mk 1 support coach leading.
Gavin Morrison

Above:
The Ivatt Class 4MT 2-6-0 to be preserved is No 43106. In early 1981, having been thoroughly restored at the Severn Valley Railway (where it continues to be based), it enjoyed several outings on the main line, being seen passing Heyford *en route* for Birmingham with a special from Didcot on 11 April. However, the locomotive has now been out of traffic for several years, awaiting expensive repairs. *Gavin Morrison*

Left:
Ivatt '2MT' 2-6-0 No 46441, is seen in a spurious maroon livery. Allowed out on the Settle & Carlisle on 24 September 1994, it performed faultlessly on the six-coach 'Westmorlander', seen emerging from the short Taitlands Tunnel at Stainforth on its journey north to Carlisle. *Gavin Morrison*